Charles L. Cingolani
In the Wheat

Charles L. Cingolani

In the Wheat

Songs in Your Presence

Haag + Herchen

Die Deutsche Bibliothek – CIP-Einheitsaufnahme

Cingolani, Charles L.:
In the wheat : songs in your presence / Charles
L. Cingolani. – Frankfurt am Main : Haag und
Herchen, 1994
    ISBN 3-86137-153-7

ISBN 3-86137-153-7
© 1994 by HAAG + HERCHEN Verlag GmbH,
Fichardstraße 30, 60322 Frankfurt am Main
Alle Rechte vorbehalten
Produktion: Herchen KG, Frankfurt am Main
Satz: W. Niederland, Frankfurt am Main
Herstellung: Prisma Druck, Frankfurt am Main
Printed in Germany

Verlagsnummer 2153

Rise up, my love, my fair
one, and come with me.
For, lo, the winter is
past, the rain is over and
gone; the flowers have
begun to blossom at home,
we can hear the turtle-dove
cooing in our land ...

Rouse thee, and come, so
beautiful, so well beloved,
still hiding thyself as a
dove hides in cleft rock or
crannied wall. Shew me but
thy face, let me but hear
thy voice, that voice sweet
as thy face is fair.

Song of Songs 2:10-14

1

When we were boys
You were
so much closer.
We could almost
touch
You,
we thought.

There were
days
when You
were
as close as
the warm gold
of candles
or
weeds
on the path
near the
lake.

2

One thing
we knew
was this:
to be
with You
we had to
leave cities
and change.
So one hundred
and twenty
came
in black
and vied
with
one another
to see
who
could serve
You
best.

3

On the
way
I saw
Ohioan
cathedrals
of
silos and trees
and orderly
homes
on farms
like churches
and
you
standing
out there
in the middle
of
the harvest.

4

You brought
us together
from the
sidewalks
of America
with our
calloused
hands
and scuffed
knees
and we
felt forlorn
and
ill at ease
in jackets
and ties
and
no one mentioned
our bicycles
left behind
or our
saddened dogs.

5

Soon
we began
to sew
tight seams
of friendship
knowing that
each of us
cherished
the same
desire:
one day
after endless
naves
of longing
to ascend
those steps
and stand
clad
as priests
before Your
altar.

6

You woke
us
from our
lethargy
fired
us
with
energy
and drove us
beyond
every
stone of
recognition
to a
garden of
intimacy
with apples
from
every
tree.

7

You were so
overwhelming
to boys
that we lost
interest
in algebra
and Greek
and
would have
fled to
darkened chapels
to dance
in panting
prayer
around Your
altars
like
minstrels
clowns
or
troubadours.

8

We would
let ourselves
fall
when
in Your
presence
and felt
you
catch us
without question
like
a basin
welcoming
water,
but
knew
the formal
usage
frowned on
that.

9

We were
taught
to walk
slowly
and
to sit
erect
with hands
resting
lightly
just above the
knees,
and not
one of us
asked
why
that
had
to
be.

10

We had to speak
to You
from black
prayer books
thumbmarked
with use
but secretly
pursued
other wordless ways
like kneeling
without moving
or sitting
with hand to head
musing
or watching
the window
kindle
with
morning light.

11

We were told
to live in
silence
like seeds have
in soil
that we might
one day
break through
and flower,
but we preferred
the silence
we found in rooms
where fragrance
breathed
from linen and wood
and were lured
to deeper spaces
by the
colors of stillness –
and forgot
about
the flowering.

12

You said
things
to us
in silence
that fell
into deep
furrows
of understanding.

So changed
were we
that
we
read in
books
to find out
what
had
happened.

13

In our minds
there was
no doubt
that You
were
near.
Can You
remember us
cascading
down long
slopes
and laughing
knowing that
You were
waiting
down
there
at the water's
edge
to catch us.

14

We never
asked
ourselves
if
we believed
it was
You
we held
in bread
on our
tongues
for
those
ten
brief
moments
of ecstatic
oneness.

15

Do You
remember
how
each of us
had
his own
special
way of
genuflecting
and
entering
the pew
without
stepping
on the
smooth
leather
matting?

16

We wondered
how
priests
who told
us about
You
could bear
to busy themselves
with things
other than
chalices
amices and
palls
and tear
themselves
away
even for an hour
from all
those
intimacies
we longed for.

17

We knew
You
expected from us
Latin
and we studied
it
to make
our tongues
say
those
words
You wanted,
but sulked
that Cicero
was
given
all that
attention
in Your
stead.

18

Often
when kneeling
I would
gaze at
the grain
in the wood
and wonder
if I had
come upon
ciphered
words
to
understand
written
boldly
in
Your
flowing hand.

19

We were just
boys
no wonder
You liked
us.

Remember how
we sat up
straight
and learned to
meditate
on You
mornings
at six
when outside
the sun
was picking
her way
up
the
tree?

20

How we learned
the countless
columns
of words
in Latin
French
and Greek
stacking them
towards You,
we masons in
Babel,
til they
fell down
around us
and we,
with dusty tongues
sat
speechless
on our
hill of
rubble.

21

You speak
a
different
language
that only
boys
burning
with fervor
can
understand
and
translate
into
hidden
silent
gestures.

22

We read
the books
of
silence
and
nothingness
and began
to understand
things
that stirred
in them
like
longing
and
fire,
and threw
the other books
away.

23

The Argonauts
couldn't fire
our imagination
because
You had
done it
before them,
and
their travels
were but a story
whereas
on our voyage
You stood
right there
on the deck
before us
and we
set sails
for wheresoever
You guided
us.

24

What kind
of swivel
was it
on which
You leashed me
so
successfully?
Ah, did You
really
want me
at Your
heels
when
all the others
were busy
learning
verb forms
and
history?

25

It was neither
swivel
nor
leash
You used
to bind –
it was some
living
cord
through which
living
morsels
of
sweetness
were
sent,
to which
I
soon
became
addicted.

You haven't
forgotten
all the
moments
I had
with You
in closed
rooms
of intimacy.

Or did You,
perhaps,
later
when
others came
who might
have learned
how to love
You
better?

There was one
among us
with high
shoulders,
Patrick by name,
who seemed
to know You
well
already
and
what You expected
so we watched
and even walked
as he,
worrying
secretly
that You might
shower him
with all
Your attentions.

Did You know
that during
a break
in games
or
just before
we served
a ball
we would
look up
past the barn
to Your
chapel,
for
just
a second?

29

Passers-by
would stop
along
the cinder
path
to watch
us
at our
spirited games
and never knew
that we
were playing for You
with
torrid
fervor
as if to win
You
over.

30

Are those
fatherly
trees
still
standing
around the
baseball
field
spreading their
branches
over the benches
where we sat
between innings
being tempted
to forsake You
for the
lights
and
distant
smoke-filled
diamonds.

31

Now I know
You
were moved
when
hungry boys
stood
patiently
at tables
with folded
arms
waiting
to say
their
distracted
grace
hastily.

32

Sometimes
while kneeling
I would
run a finger
over
the soft stubble
at my ear
or glance
at the
hairs
on my hand
and wonder
what
that
meant.

33

Did You
notice
how
after
we had lost
ourselves
in You
so many
things
ceased to
upset us
like when
the pine
was struck
right
outside
the
study hall?

34

There was
one
priest
we especially
esteemed
who spent
all
his
time
walking
back and forth
quietly
under
the
trees.

35

At night
in dreams
we took
on wings
and
flew
with ease
from
tree to tree
along
the path
where
priests
would say
their
breviary.

36

There were
times
when
everything
was
so
peaceful
that I would
sit
and
dream about
some trial
to suit me
and
be seen
with.

37

Silence
was
a columned
hall
of
order
we
sat
in
and expanded
beyond
the boundaries
of
boundless
open
spaces.

38

I felt comfortable
near pendulums
of time
wheezing in
clocks
counting
strokes from
steeples
across lakes
and would lie
there
thinking
how
tidy days
could
pass
on wings
through quiet
rooms
of scheduled
order.

39

Who ever
counted
our
myriad
passages
through
the
silent
confines
of
corridors
and
halls
in ordered
rhythmic
traffic
over
porous
yellow
tiles?

40

How unencumbered
we were
when we came
to You,
like blank
tablets
like unchiseled
stones
not even knowing
what kings were,
were it not for books,
and we had
but one sun
and she
ran her course
up over
our measured span
of Indiana
trees.

41

You
penetrated
our
narrow
spaces
boldly
with
glistening
swords
of
slanted
sunlight
and
we felt
spurred
by
Your
brazen
flourishes.

42

Our hours
passed
on schedules
of unchanging
ritual
attuning us
to rhythms
distant
and
regular
like
the tides
or
the arcing
of the sun
above
our scorched
window sills.

43

After all
these years
the thought arises
You might recall
those
hidden winces
of homesickness
when,
after train rides
across the night
our ways
wound back
to a crib
we knelt at
before
a blurred
plaster figure
on straw
under
half-naked
pines.

How it hurt
on rainy
days
to kneel
alone
and happen
to see
an empty
tackmark
on the wall
where
a Christmas
wreath
had
hung.

45

And all
during
those
years
minutes
were being
measured
diligently
by the onlooking
clock
in low
swinging
arcs
there
on that
wall
where
all our
corridors
met.

46

They
grounded
us
in the
French
traditions,
talked quietly
and tended to
us
like plants
but
never
stopped
to think
how
different
our soil
was:

For we were
the children
of unschooled
Shawnees
Potawatamis
and
Miamis
who
had walked
on those
selfsame
plains
with
a piety
that
still seeped
from the
fields
to infect us.

48

Why did they
teach me
to refrain
my innocent
complaisance
that took You
as my friend
on a familiar
basis?
When someone
told me
to be strong
and not expect
Your warm
affections
I thought
how
incongruous
that was.

49

We loved
You
for no
reason
other
than
that
we
wanted
to.

50

For we
came
to
You
with
full
volition
that
was
older
than
we
and
had
been
stirring
in us
since
we were
three.

51

We tried
so hard
to learn discipline
in those
young years
when
emotions welled
like never
before
or since
but
with time
we learned
to rein them
in,
even if
we somehow felt
that
part of us
was missing.

52

When they
talked
about
formation
of habits
to gain
Your favor
we listened.
But
we knew
that
repetition alone
would
deprive
us
of all our
pent up
inventiveness.

53

They were
careful
to make
us
aware
of tradition
but You
gave us
our own
intuition
and we,
in our
simplicity,
wooed
You
with dogged
boyish
ineptitude.

54

After a while
those
whose
students
we were
perceived
there was
no further
need
for us
to be conditioned
to Your
service,
so they
went
over
to bridling.

55

We didn't
sleep
on briars
but when
we
wanted to
they gave
us
blankets
instead.

56

When we
passed
them
on the
path
didn't the flowers
sense
the
intensity
of our
piety
and say
they had
found
partners
in
rendering
You
worship?

57

We hardly
knew
what to do
with all
the inner life
You gave us
and would
sometimes
climb
over walls
and into nature,
kept at a distance
to our dismay
for fear
she might
afford
some
corresponding
abundance.

But for
those walls
we were set
in a landscape
of fields
and woods
and would have
celebrated
their rhythms
and
rituals
like hermits did
but
our rules
applied to
cenobites
who had left
the fields
outside
to be worked at
and utilized.

59

Every thing
spoke
to us
about You
in a
fresh
and pristine
way
and even we
saw
that
You were *new*
like each dawning
day,
and we felt
You wore
the musty
clothes they had You
wear
unwillingly.

60

You were
not
someone
we learned
to imagine
from
superb creations
we had
grown up with
like
Chartres
or Cologne,
and the paintings
hadn't reached us yet,
no,
we experienced
You
new,
like birds do
or the walled in
girl
of Lisieux.

61

You
remained
plain
for us,
coarse
and unprepared
even
for the majesty
of Hadyn,
for
You knew
we would have been
blinded
had You
thrust
too much
light
on us
at once.

62

You saved
us
from the
weight
of art,
that subjugates –
but
You
subdued
us
with
Your
gentility.

63

You were
never
mean
with us,
other rules
governed
than those of
harshness.
When we
thought
You might
punish us
You never did,
and tears,
welled up
at
feeling
what
gentleness
was.

64

We never
cringed
before You,
never
felt the
need to,
knowing
that You
saw
more
in each
of us
than
all the
others.

65

You made
us
proud
to be ourselves
and
when
admonished
to confess
our sins
to appease You
we asked
sincerely
if
we had
ever done
anything
to displease
You.

66

We had
a unique
orientation
with the
insights
You
gave us
and felt
that we
should
see to it
that
You
derive
Your
daily bread
from us,
and not we
ours
from
You.

67

I can remember
thinking
it just
wasn't like
You
to promise
us things
to make us
be good
so I once
asked
innocently
if someone
had
made up
the idea of
heaven
for You.

68

We wanted
to hear
someone
tell us
about
You
but
they
always
talked
on Your
periphery,
as if
to keep
us
from
boring.

69

On thinking back
I remember
You
as being
young
and dark
and somehow
weak,
which was
irresistably
attractive,
and what was more
You were
near,
as if
in a
room
next to mine,
alone
and waiting.

70

It was as if
You had torn down
all the limits
except for
that one thin wall
between us
where we lingered
insisting
we wanted over,
but
You didn't banish us
for wanting
knowledge
but went right on
squandering
liberties
on us
regardless,
or was it
because of,
our
undaunted
hankering.

71

There were
robins
nesting at
the infirmary
window
when I was
sick
and had planned
to enjoy
being alone
with You,
but I spent
all my time
at the window
getting better
without
feeling
I had
slighted
You
whatsoever.

When You
kept
me
behind
the thin
glass
of distance
how did
You
stand
my repeated
query
as to why
You
were abusing
me
so thoroughly?

73

And
didn't You
grow
tired
of my
constant
plea
for
help
in geometry?

74

What compass
could we
ever
have
used
to see
us
through
the flood
tides
of Your
generosities
over
all
those
years?

75

Had we been born
five years
earlier
we would have had
to crawl out
on the battlefields
of war
but there
we were
sitting quiet
reading
about soldiers
who had returned
to wall
themselves
in cloisters
and their
abandon
fired ours
all the
more.

76

Could it
be
that You
spoiled
us
like no others
because
a War
had just been
waged
and even
You
needed
boyish
consolation
during
those
distorted
days?

We ached
to be
monks
in white
cowls
and
contemplate,
unaware
that
then and there
You were
treating
us
to favors
that seasoned
monks
had never
tasted.

78

And time
ran
straight
down
through
our
days
like
a
gurgling
brook
through
a
lush
green
lawn.

Where is
the shiny
little
tuning fork
they used
to launch
us on
our charted
course
to distant
depths
on tidy
swells
of
flowing
chant.

Remember how
I thought
a proper
goal
for me
would be
to be
a saint,
›to Your greater
glory‹?
Even then
I felt
You smile
at me,
conniving
with words
while
praying
to You
from
my semantic
subterfuge.

She taught
us to
speak to
You,
Thérèse of Lisieux,
whose words
we wrote
in thin
black
notebooks
and spoke
when You came
close
and ours
would fail us,
for hers
brought order to
our unwieldy
ardor.

82

When
we
walked out
the path
and stood
by the
iron pickets
where the
crosses lay
did we
rely on
routine
prayers
for
something
to say?

I was disappointed
when I found
You lived
in Barock
churches.

Didn't You
feel more
at home
in our
chapel of wood
with no
other
columned
grandeur
than the
plump leg
of Your
plain
altar?

Can You
remember
the rainy
Saturday morning
I sat alone
leafing
through folios
of French
cathedrals,
worried
between pages
that
You might
feel more content
somewhere
other than
there
with us
on our plain
Indiana
farmland?

85

We had
all the order
of the Parthenon
within
those walls
for
You hewed
into our
dimensions
the pillars
of Your
presence.
How could we
have ever
seen
that our poor
yellow
bricks
were crumbling?

86

How could
we
with all our
boyish
energy
be so allured
by tranquility
were it not
for You
Whom
we found
one day
like a fawn
lying
in the wheat –
and on the spot
we pledged
to adopt
and keep
You
in a hidden
solitude.

We lived
in deep ravines
of silence
and solitude
with You
while the rhythmic
traffic
of the day
circled on ledges
at heights
far removed,
and the sun
would find its way
into our clearing
through quivering
leaves
leaving us
to enjoy
You
without
fearing
any intrusion.

88

We prayed
best
without words.
It was as
though we
knelt there
gazing
into a
pool
which was
Your
circle
and would
let
ourselves
stream in
and mingle
without making
the slightest
ripple.

We felt the weight
of Your
hovering presence
pressing lightly
over us
like low-slung
branches
that hollowed out
space
to curve down
around us
on pillarless
suspension
enclosing
sacredness
in ways
architects
had never achieved
with arches,
vaults
and traceries.

90

It wasn't
a shudder
that went
through
us, no,
a piercing
of blades
was
the bliss
that we felt
when
of a sudden
You came
and
stood
right there
beside us
like a person.

91

On those
rare
occasions
when I sat
in Your presence
in silent awe
and shuddered
wasn't I
hearing lines
of Bach Variations
which
when first heard
decades later
brought
to vibration
the elation
I had known
in those young
years.

Would we have
only been reminded
of what we had
seen
in the fields
had
our eyes ever
feasted on
a painting
by Sisley
or
could he
have taken us
out into a landscape,
like You did,
to pierce us
with Your
searing
beauty?

93

It was hard
not
to need
You
with
everything
divested
and
no one
else
to flee to.
That was when
we embraced
the specters,
thinking
we saw
You
everywhere.

Once I
fell in love
with a tree
I could
see
on a distant
field
outside
the cloister
wall.
In summer
it stood
alone
by the wheat
but
in winter
it would
lean away from
me,
modestly.

95

We cupped each
day
in seamless
hands
but poured it out
at night
to begin
anew
our playful
search
for You
Whom
we could never
catch,
even when
You broke through
our vigilancy
with bold
forays
into our
circle.

96

We were
teenaged
boys,
rough-edged
selfish
torrid
proud
and yet
You held us
dear
and pierced us
with years
of
sweet
injuries
that never
healed.

97

Later
we wore
cinctures
and felt
some deep
moat
encircling
us
like
castles
must,
or lovers
when
once
smitten.

98

How many poems
have mothers
sighed
to You
from their
beds of labour
when the
pain
subsides?
What words
do monks
find
evenings
in August
when lying
on pallets
of straw
while
outside
the hay
is drying
in the fields?

If only
it could be still
again
like it was
on winter
afternoons
at
twenty minutes
past five
when
the day seemed
to have laid down
arms
before
entering into
the
truce tent
of night.

100

Can You still
hear
how
the groups
of lively boys
talking
under the
trees
by the
semicircular
bench
would allow
the silence
to settle in
once the bell
had rung
for
evening prayer?

101

In rooms
where candles
burn
I remember
long
dark
Saturday afternoons
with taut exercises
in prayer,
candelabras
linens
and air
that moved
slowly,
drenching us
with incense
and
desire.

Do you remember
the warm evening
You came
and sat
with me
for
ten minutes
just
inside
the stone wall
of
the apple orchard
until
the sun
had gone down
behind
the silent
New England
woods?

103

Where is
the place
where I
can stand
in gothic
composure
and be
elevated
to You
in
one long
vertical
thrust
of breathless
blind
desire?

104

Now,
every thing is new again.
Spring has blossomed quietly
across the plains.
Already I can hear You
coming into the wheat
looking for him
who once found You there.
After the winter
was over, You said.
Nothing has meaning now
but waiting.
Come to the center
of that boundless golden field.
Come to where I have kept
You while You've been gone.
Come.
For stillness and silence
will hide our
helplessness,
in our hidden solitude.